I Got a Pet!

My Pet Guinea Pig

By Brienna Rossiter

www.littlebluehousebooks.com

Copyright © 2023 by Little Blue House, Mendota Heights, MN 55120. All rights reserved. No part of this book may be reproduced or utilized in any form or by any means without written permission from the publisher.

Little Blue House is distributed by North Star Editions:
sales@northstareditions.com | 888-417-0195

Produced for Little Blue House by Red Line Editorial.

Photographs ©: Shutterstock Images, cover, 4, 7, 8–9, 10, 13, 14–15, 16, 18–19, 21 (top), 21 (bottom), 23, 24 (top left), 24 (top right), 24 (bottom left), 24 (bottom right)

Library of Congress Control Number: 2022901882

ISBN
978-1-64619-589-3 (hardcover)
978-1-64619-616-6 (paperback)
978-1-64619-668-5 (ebook pdf)
978-1-64619-643-2 (hosted ebook)

Printed in the United States of America
Mankato, MN
082022

About the Author

Brienna Rossiter is a writer and editor who lives in Minnesota.

Table of Contents

My Pet Guinea Pig **5**

Playtime **11**

Guinea Pig Care **17**

Glossary **24**

Index **24**

My Pet Guinea Pig

I have a guinea pig.

It is a very good pet.

My guinea pig lives in a cage.
Shavings cover the cage's floor.
They make the floor soft.

The cage has a hut where my guinea pig can hide. Sometimes it pokes its head out.

Playtime

I take my guinea pig out of its cage to play with it.
I hold it gently.

I love to pet my guinea pig.
It has soft fur.

Sometimes I let my guinea pig run on the floor.

It moves quickly.

Guinea Pig Care

I keep my guinea pig's cage clean.

I give it cardboard to chew.

My guinea pig eats pellets and seeds.

I put its food in a bowl.

My guinea pig eats other foods, too.

It eats vegetables.

It also eats hay and grass.

My guinea pig drinks from
a water bottle.
I make sure the bottle
stays full.